READING FOR THE CONTEMPORARY GUITARIST

Volume 3

IAN ROBBINS

Library of Congress Cataloging-in-Publication Data
Name: Robbins, Ian Matthew, author.
Title: Reading for the Contemporary Guitarist Volume 2/ Ian Robbins
Identifiers: LCCN TXu2209262 | ISBN 9781732996861 (paperback) | ISBN 9781732996878

ISBN: 9781732996847 (paperback)
ISBN: 9781732996854 (ebook)

Table of Contents

Chapter 1: Combining Positions I-VII, Two String Horizontal Reading, and Cut Time

Wide Range Reading

The following exercises will contain ranges too large for just one position. Using the keys as your guide, try these examples using any combination of positions I-VII:

1.1

1.2

1.3

1.4

1.5

1.6

1.7

1.8

1.9

1.10

1.11

3

1.12

1.13

1.14

1.15

1.16

1.17

1.18

1.19

1.20

1.21

Read the following examples horizontally using ONLY the indicated strings:

1st and 2nd Strings

1.22

2nd and 3rd Strings

1.23

3rd and 4th Strings

1.24

4th and 5th Strings

1.25

5th and 6th Strings

1.26

6th and 4th Strings

1.27

5th and 3rd Strings

1.28

4th and 2nd Strings

1.29

3rd and 1st Strings

1.30

The indicator for a cut time signature appears as follows:

Which is equivalent to

This means the half note becomes the pulse, thereby doubling the values as they would relate in 4/4 (common time).

The following examples would be identical rhythmically:

1.31

The reason for cut time is to <u>simplify</u> faster passages of music. It should help relax your feel as your foot would only be tapping half the amount as if you were to play the congruent figure in 4/4 time.

Try the following cut time examples in any position you would like:

1.32

1.33

1.34

1.35

1.36

1.37

1.38

12

1.39

1.40

1.41

1.42

1.43

1.44

1.45

Assignment:

BUDGET CUT

Chapter 2: Introduction to Position VIII, Cut Time Cont., Eighth Note Triplet Syncopation, and Natural Harmonics

Notes in Position VIII

Examine position VIII and its potential fingerings:

2.1

The fingerings here are given in terms of a chromatic scale. It would be perfectly acceptable to use the fingering you find the most comfortable to help construct a good flow for a given musical passage. In the following exercises the fingering choices will be left up to you. Make sure to stay in position VIII as you play these passages:

C Major

2.2

2.3

The exercises below will call upon keys that are ideal for position VIII.

Ab Major

2.4

2.5

2.6

2.7

F Minor

2.8

2.9

2.10

19

2.11

Db Major

2.12

2.13

2.14

2.15

Bb Minor

2.16

2.17

2.18

2.19

Cut Time Reading with Ties

Perform the rhythmic examples until comfortable, then the next example which will feature identical rhythms with moving pitches. Choose the position that best matches the range and key:

2.20

2.21

2.22

2.23

2.24

2.25

2.26

2.27

Eighth Note Triplet Syncopation

If playing eighth note triplets you have to consider either a reset of your pick on strong beats, or flipping the pick to an upstroke one the second group:

2.28

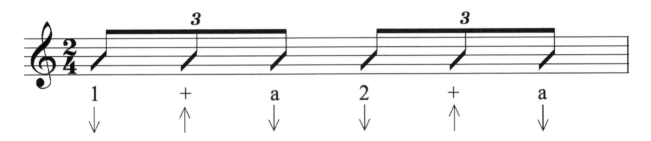

Or:

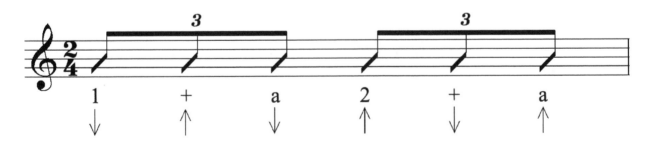

I would suggest the reset (top) approach in most cases. If you are playing constant triplets at faster speeds, the alternating (bottom) approach might be more feasible. When eighth note triplets are separated by holds or rests, I would recommend playing the first attack with a down pick and the second attack with an up pick no matter where the rhythm breaks. This will allow for an easier reset to the downbeat and aligning better with your foot tap. Here are a few examples of this concept:

2.29

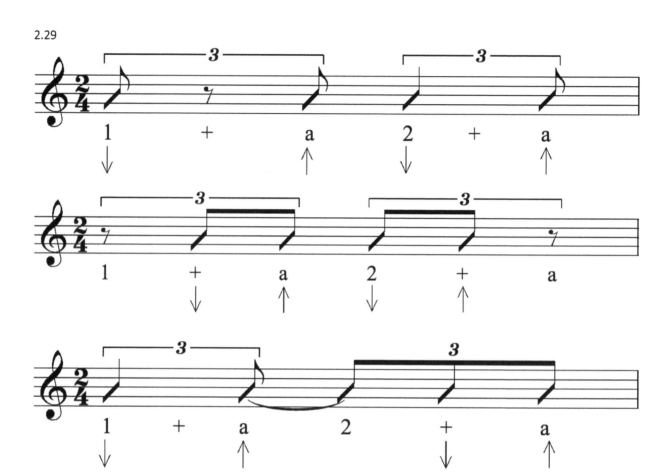

Try out this strategy in the following exercises. Perform the rhythmic examples until comfortable, then the next example which will feature identical rhythms with moving pitches. Choose the position that best matches the range and key:

2.30

*If there is only one attack in the triplet group, use a downwards pick for beat 1 or an upwards pick for both the '+' and 'a'.

2.31

2.32

2.33

2.34

2.35

2.36

2.37

Reading Articulations: Natural Harmonics

There are two ways of indicating a natural harmonic in guitar notation. The first would be to indicate the finger position of where the left hand would sound the harmonic and place an "o" symbol above it. The second would be to indicate the placement of the left hand with a diamond head notation.

2.37

Natural Harmonics on the Twelfth Fret

2.38

Natural Harmonics on the Seventh Fret

The harmonics on the Seventh and Twelfth fret produce a pitch an octave higher than written. The same harmonic series on the seventh fret also exists on the nineteenth fret except here the pitches sound in the same register. On the fifth fret, the harmonics produced are different pitches than the note would be if fretted normally. You might see the sounding pitch above the fretted pitch written in parenthesis. The pitch will be a twelfth (an octave plus a fifth) above the fret position.

2.39

Natural Harmonics on the Fifth Fret

There are of course other places to play natural harmonics such as, slightly behind the 4th or 2nd frets. Those would be written in a similar fashion, with the fret being considered the notated pitch.

Read the following exercises and perform natural harmonics when indicated:

2.40

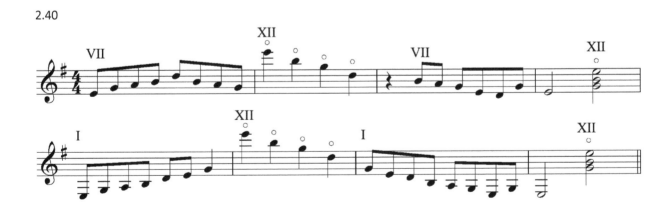

28

2.41

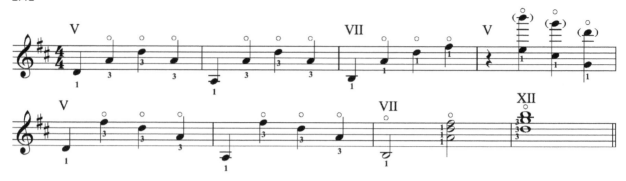

2.42

2.43

Assignment:

Harm Onyx

Chapter 3: Position VIII Cont., Eighth Note Triplet Syncopation Cont., and Position VII 8va Review.

Read the following examples in position VIII:

Eb Major

3.1

3.2

3.3

3.4

3.5

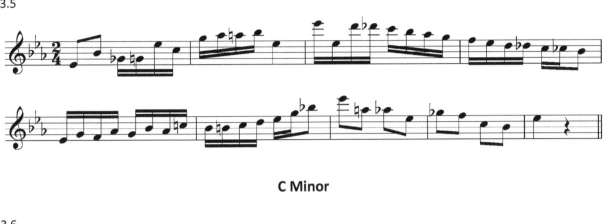

C Minor

3.6

3.7

3.8

3.9

3.10

B Major

3.11

3.12

3.13

3.14

3.15

G# Minor

3.16

3.17

3.18

3.19

3.20

These exercises will combine eighth and sixteenth note rhythms with the syncopated eighth note triplet figures from the previous chapter. Be diligent in switching your subdivisions earlier than the upcoming figure whenever possible. For example:

3.21

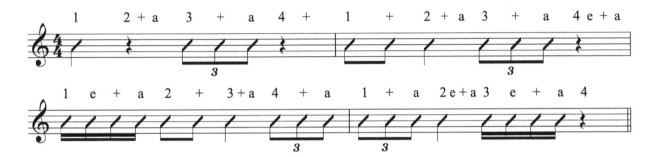

When you have a quarter note figure or rest you should start subdividing whatever rhythm group is next. There will be plenty of situations where you don't have this luxury but getting in the habit of doing this will help train your mind for sections where the subdivision changes in each beat. The more syncopated the figure, the more important this practice becomes.

Try to apply this method throughout these examples. Read in any position:

3.22

3.23

3.24

3.25

3.26

3.27

3.28

3.29

3.30

3.31

3.32

3.33

Position VII 8va Review:

Read the following examples in position VII one octave higher than written. Try to push the tempos on these:

3.34

3.35

3.40

3.41

3.42

Don't Trip

Chapter 4: Position VIII continued, Position VII and VIII combined, Review Exercises

Read the following examples in position VIII:

Gb Major

Eb Minor

4.4

4.5

4.6

F# Major

4.7

4.8

4.9

D# Minor

4.10

4.11

Use positions VII and/or VIII to create the smoothest fingerings through the following passages:

4.12

4.13

4.14

4.15

Read the following examples in positions I and/or II:

4.21

4.22

4.23

4.24

4.25

4.26

Syncopation Review Exercises

Read the single note example until comfortable. The exercise that follows will contain duplicate rhythms with melodic and harmonic detail. Read in any position:

4.27

4.28

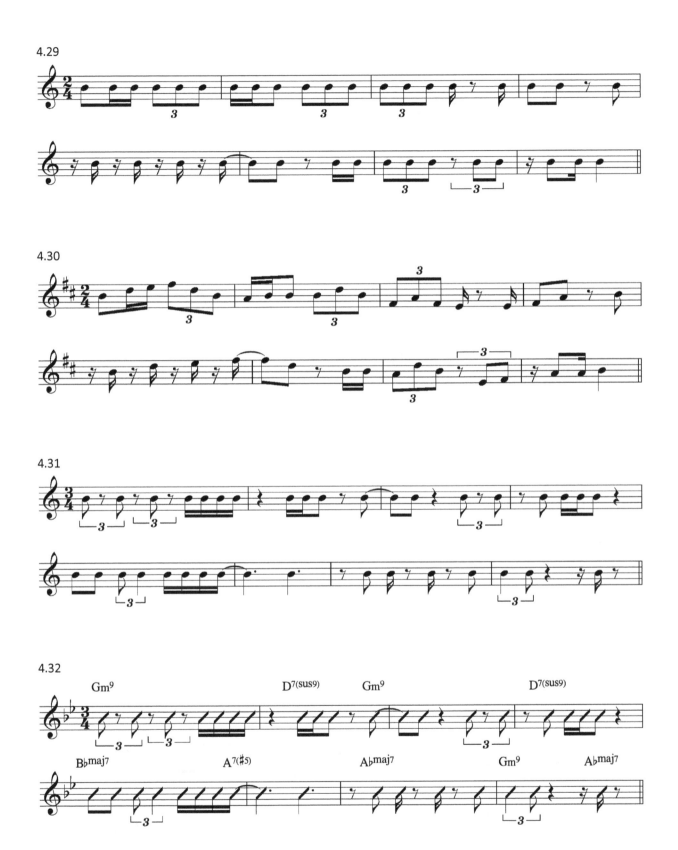

4.33

4.34

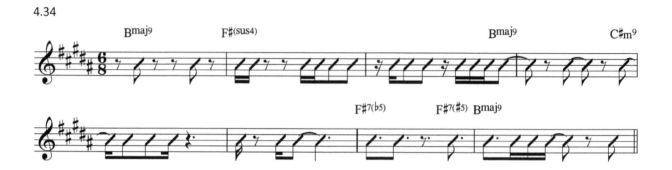

Articulation Review Exercises

Read the following exercises in any position(s) you choose. Make sure to follow all indicated articulations:

4.35

4.36

Assignment:

Choose your reading position based on ease of fingerings and ability to control written articulations. You do not need to stay fixed in any one position.

Jury Duty

57

Chapter 5: Introduction to Position IX, Eighth Note Triplet Syncopation Cont., and Chordal Reading in Position I

Notes in Position IX

Examine position IX and its potential fingerings:

5.1

The fingerings here are given in terms of a chromatic scale. As before, it would be perfectly acceptable to use the fingering you find the most comfortable to help construct a good flow for a given musical passage. Make sure to stay in position IX as you play these passages:

D Major

5.2

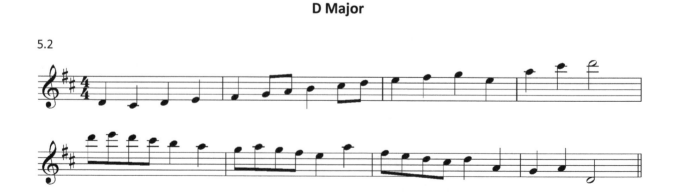

B Minor

5.11

A Major

5.12

5.13

5.14

5.15

5.16

F# Minor

5.17

5.18

5.19

5.20

5.21

Tied Eighth Note Triplet Syncopation Exercises

The following rhythmic examples feature tied eighth note triplet rhythms. Perform them until comfortable using the pick directions established in earlier units. The second example of each pair which will feature identical rhythms with moving pitches. Choose the position that best matches the range and key:

5.22

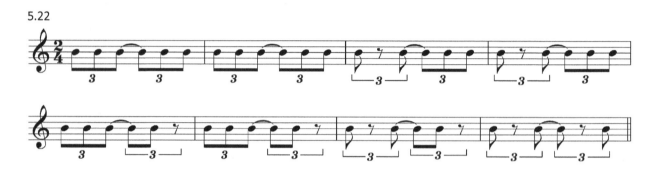

5.23

5.24

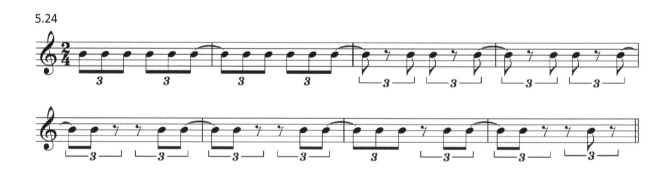

5.25

5.26

5.27

5.28

66

5.29

5.30

5.31

Chordal Reading Position I

Use your knowledge of how to visualize intervals on the staff as you try to read these four-part chord voicings in position I:

5.32

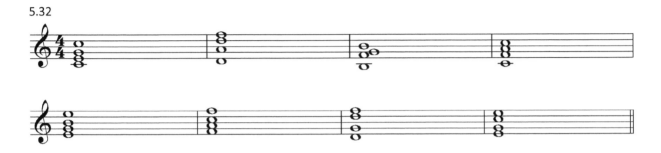

5.33

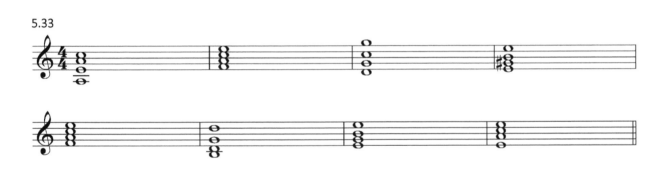

5.34

5.35

5.36

5.37

5.38

5.39

5.40

Assignment:

STREIGHTH NOTES

D.C. AL CODA
(NO REPEATS)

Chapter 6: Position IX Cont., Quarter Note Triplet Syncopation, and Chordal Reading in Positions II and V

Play the following exercises in position IX:

G Major

6.1

6.2

6.3

6.4

6.5

E Minor

6.6

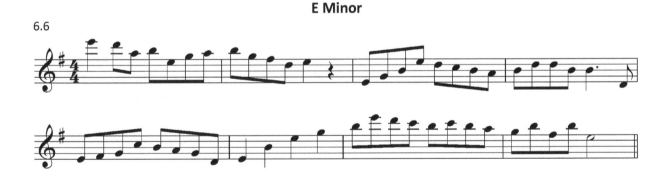

6.7

74

6.8

6.9

6.10

E Major

6.11

6.12

6.13

6.14

6.15

C# Minor

6.16

6.17

6.18

6.19

6.20

Quarter Note Triplet Syncopation

When counting quarter note triplets, especially at slower tempos, it is imperative to count via an eighth note triplet subdivision. Remember that each attack on a quarter note triplet is equal to the length of two eighth note triplets tied together:

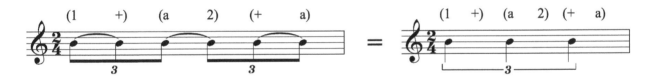

To develop an accurate sense of this concept, tap your foot on 1 and 2, play the eighth note triplet subdivision with the indicated pick directions and clap the quarter note triplet:

6.21

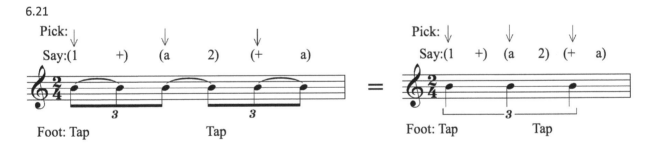

Try doing all down picks here, since the attacks are evenly spaced. This should give an even approach to the rhythm. You may also consider reading in cut time and so that the count of the quarter note triplet becomes identical to how you have been counting eighth note triplets up to this point. Try the rhythmic exercises below using either of these concepts:

6.22

80

6.32

6.33

6.34

6.35

Chordal Reading Position II

Read these four-part chord voicings in position II:

6.36

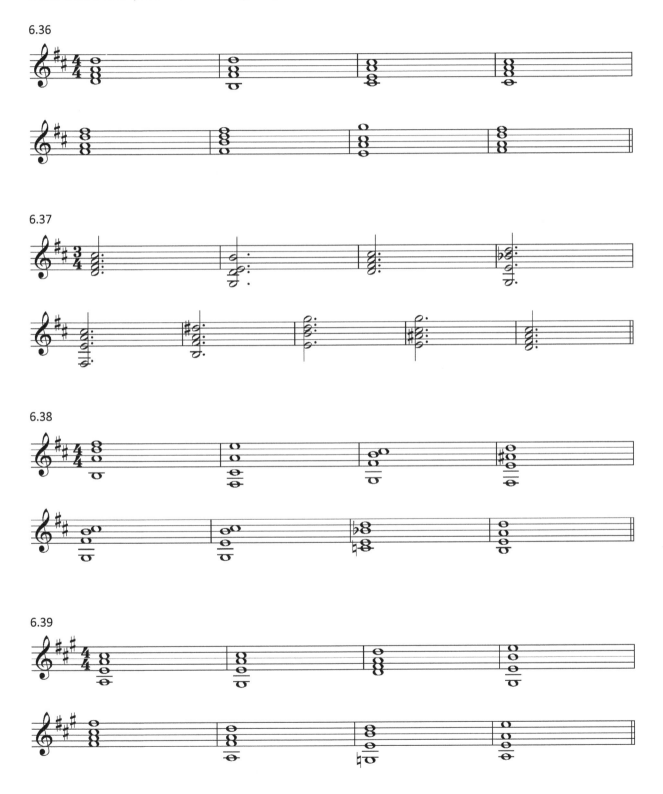

6.37

6.38

6.39

6.40

6.41

6.42

Chordal Reading Position V

Read these four-part chord voicings in position V:

6.43

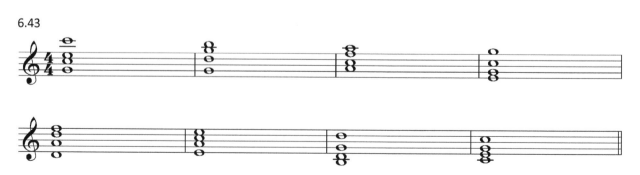

6.44

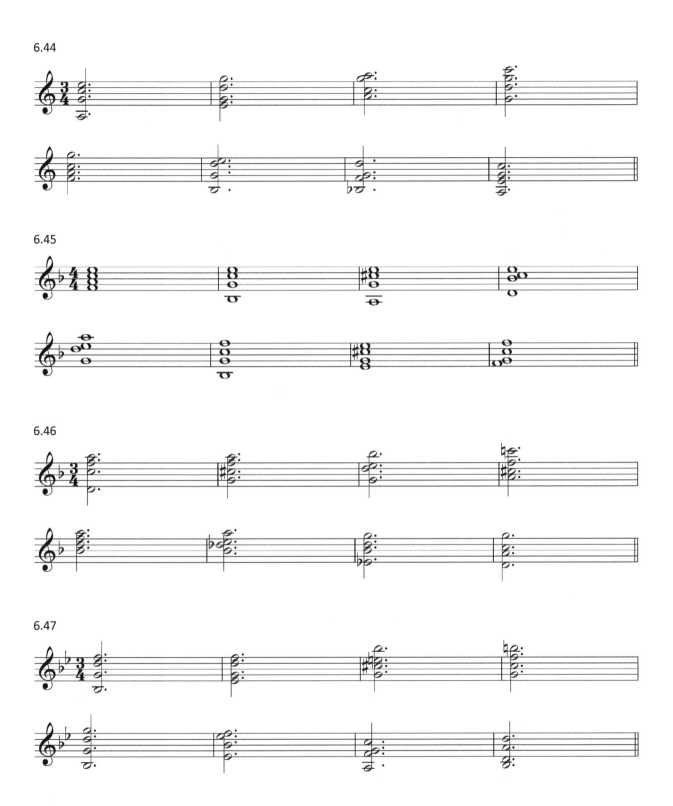

6.45

6.46

6.47

Assignment:

Chord Stack Fever

Chapter 7: Position IX Cont., Comprehensive Review Exercises

Play the following exercises in position IX:

C Major

A Minor

Position VII 8va Review

Read the following exercises and octave higher than written in position VII:

7.11

7.12

7.13

7.14

7.15

7.16

Cut Time Review Exercises

The examples should be read at faster tempos. Use any position(s) you feel comfortable in:

7.21

7.22

7.23

7.24

7.25

7.26

7.27

7.28

7.29

7.30

7.31

Articulation Review Exercises
Read the following examples using positions VII-IX. Focus on executing the written articulations:

7.32

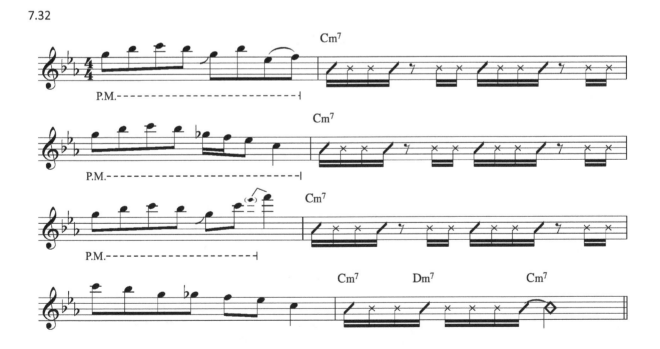

7.33

7.34

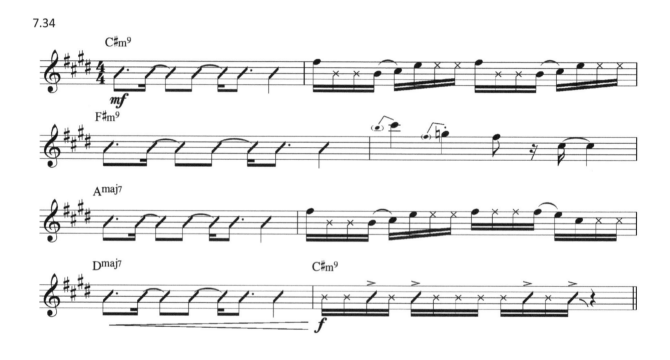

7.35

7.36

7.37

Assignment:

Kneel Young

Chapter 8: Introduction to Position X, Quarter and Eighth Note Triplet Syncopation Cont., and Chordal Reading Cont.

Notes in Position X

Examine position X and its potential fingerings:

8.1

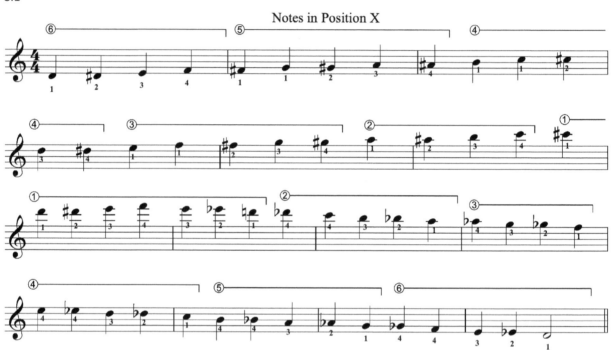

The fingerings here are given in terms of a chromatic scale. As before, it would be perfectly acceptable to use the fingering you find the most comfortable to help construct a good flow for a given musical passage. Make sure to stay in position X as you play these passages:

Bb Major

8.2

8.3

8.4

8.5

8.6

100

G Minor

8.7

8.8

8.9

8.10

8.11

8.12

Eb Major

8.13

8.14

8.15

8.16

C Minor

8.17

8.18

8.19

8.20

8.21

Tied Quarter and Eighth Note Triplet Syncopation Exercises

The following rhythmic examples feature tied eighth note triplet rhythms. Perform them until comfortable using the pick directions established in earlier units. The second example of each pair which will feature identical rhythms with moving pitches. Choose the position that best matches the range and key:

8.22

8.23

8.24

8.25

8.26

8.27

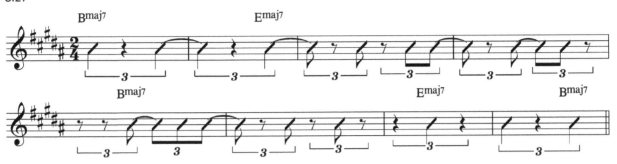

8.28

8.29

8.30

8.31

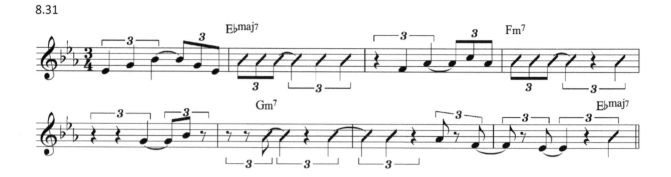

Chordal Reading Positions I, II, and V

Look at each chord individually to find the position. Choose from positions I, II and/or V:

8.32

8.33

8.34

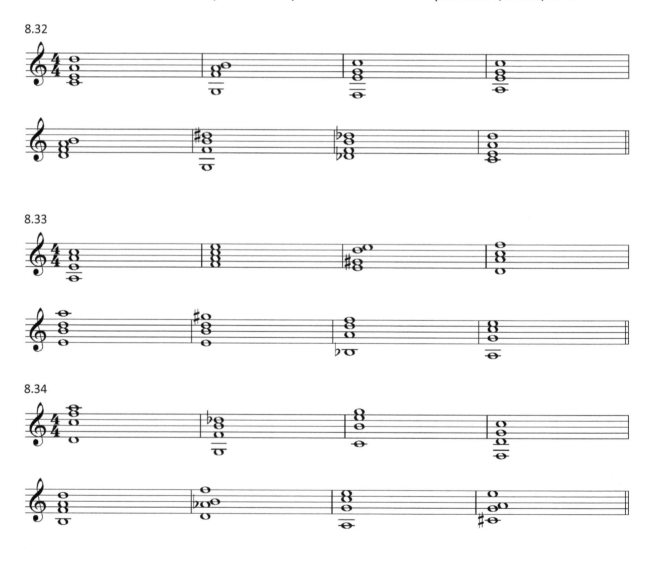

8.35

8.36

8.37

8.38

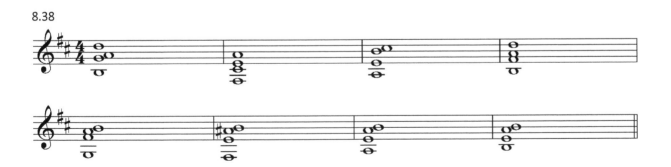

8.39

8.40

This page has been left blank intentionally

Assignment:

Gauze Pile

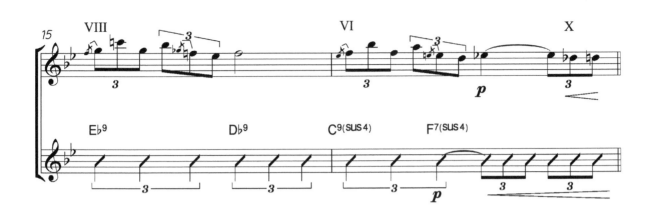

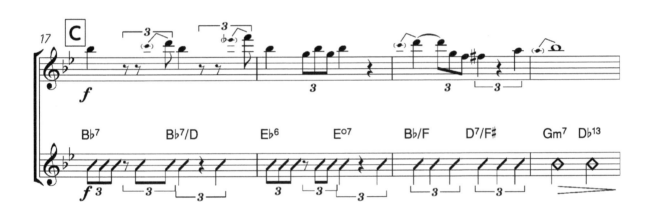

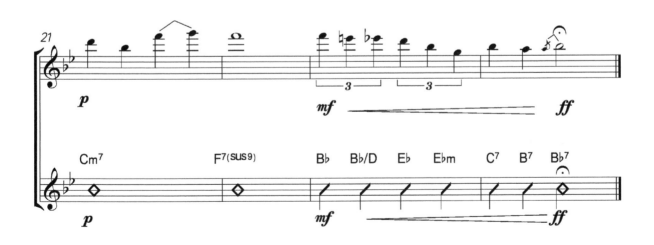

Chapter 9: Position X Cont., Rock Articulations, and Review Exercises

Play the following exercises in position X:

F Major

9.1

9.2

9.3

9.4

9.5

D Minor

9.6

9.7

9.8

114

9.9

9.10

9.11

Ab Major

9.12

9.13

9.14

9.15

F Minor

9.16

9.17

9.18

9.19

9.20

Rock Guitar Articulations

A lot of rock music, when written out, is written in TABs. However, it is possible to write out specific rock articulations in standard notation:

Vibrato

Tapping

Here is an example of a tap and pull off:

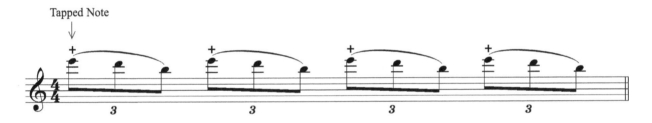

The following tap and slide would take place with only a single pick stroke:

You might also encounter a two-finger tap:

Artificial Harmonics

There are three types of artificial harmonic techniques you may see notated; *Finger Harmonics, Pinch Harmonics, and Tap Harmonics*:

Finger Harmonics

This type of harmonic is performed by very lightly touching against a note exactly twelve frets higher than the note the left hand finger is pressing. There are two ways to do this, either by touching with the index finger of the right hand and plucking the string with the ring finger or touching the string with the index finger of the right hand and plucking with the thumb. Finger harmonics are written as follows:

Pinch Harmonics

A pinch harmonic occurs when you turn your pick perpendicular to the string and bend the thumb of your right hand so that it slightly touches the string at the same time as your pick. Depending on the position of the right hand on the string, different pitches can be produced. It can be difficult to achieve this harmonic without an electric guitar on the bridge pickup, a high gain sound on the amp, and a lot of vibrato. The lower pitch will be the fretted note and the higher pitch will be the sounding note from the harmonic:

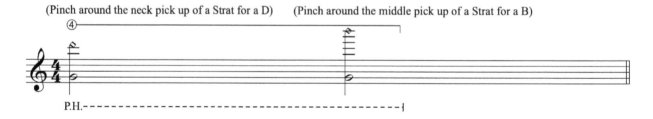

Tap Harmonics

Tap harmonics are achieved by bouncing a finger of your right hand off the string twelve frets higher than the fingered pitch. These also work better with a high gain sound:

Try the following examples on the bridge pick-up with a high gain sound:

9.21

9.22

9.23

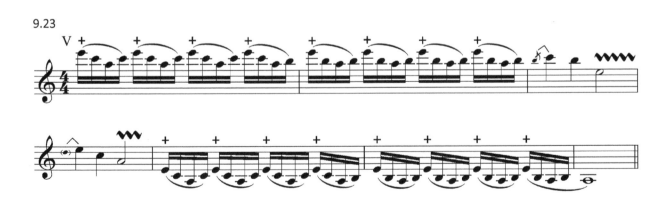

9.24

9.25

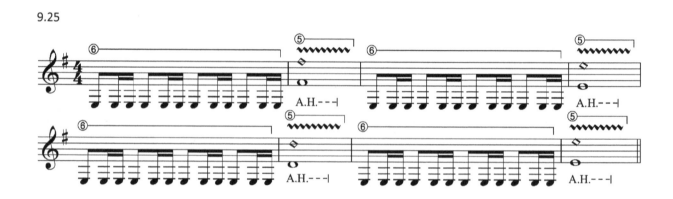

121

Chordal Reading Positions I, II, and V

Look at each chord individually to find the position:

9.26

9.27

9.28

9.29

9.30

9.31

9.32

9.33

9.34

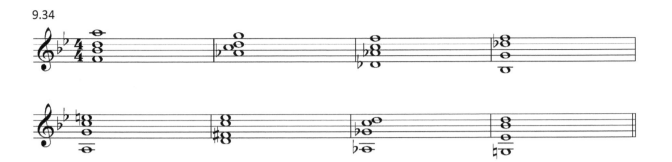

9.35

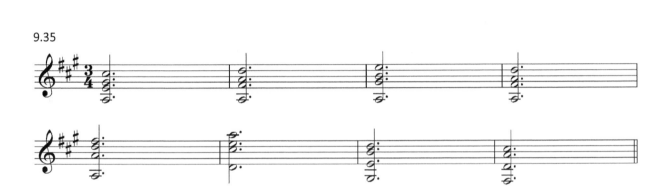

Artificial Intelligence

126

Chapter 10: Position X Cont., Position X 8va, Combining Positions, Comprehensive Review

Play the following exercises in position X:

Db Major

10.1

10.2

10.3

10.4

10.5

Bb Minor

10.6

10.7

10.8

10.9

10.10

Position X 8va

Read the following exercises and octave higher than written in position X:

10.11

10.12

10.13

10.14

10.15

10.16

Try to combine positions to facilitate the easiest fingering passage through the following exercises:

10.21

10.22

10.23

10.24

10.25

10.26

10.27

10.28

10.29

10.30

Triplet Reading Review Exercises

Read the following examples using any position you choose:

10.31

10.32

10.33

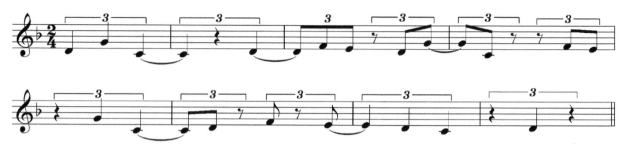

10.34

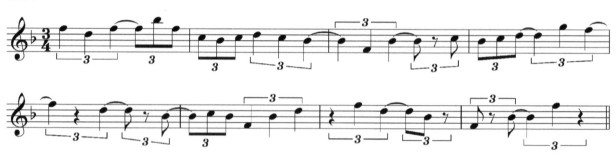

10.35

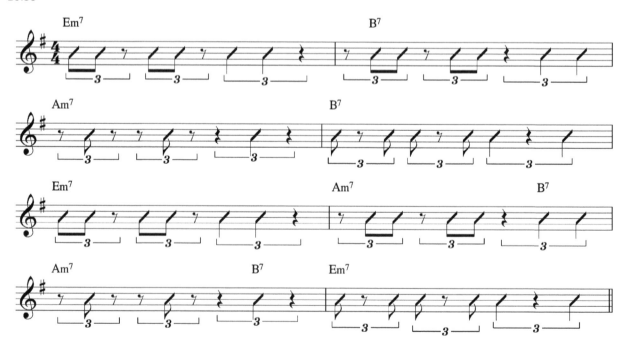

10.36

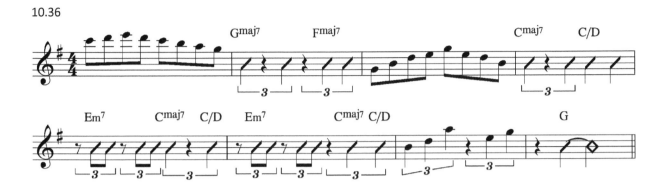

10.37

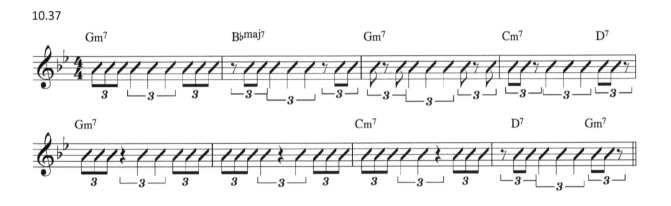

10.38

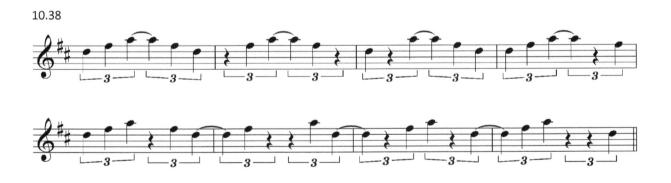

10.39

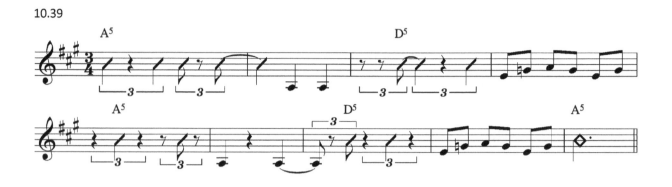

10.40

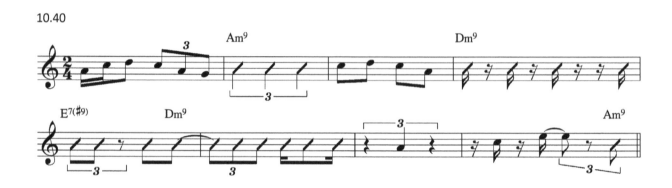

Missin' Some Teeth

Dr. Squealgood

Lightning Source UK Ltd.
Milton Keynes UK
UKHW031941090223
416682UK00011B/570